MILK and HONEY COOKING SCHOOL

Learning the History of God's People Through Cooking and Eating

Daphna Flegal
and
LeeDell Stickler

Milk and Honey Cooking School

ISBN: 978-0-687-49829-1

Writers: Daphna Flegal and LeeDell Stickler
Editor: LeeDell Stickler
Production Editor: David Whitworth
Production and Design Manager: R.E. Osborne
Cover and interior design: Paige Easter

07 08 09 10 11 12 13 14 15—10 9 8 7 6 5 4 3 2

MANUFACTURED IN THE UNITED STATES OF AMERICA

CONTENTS

INTRODUCTION

Have you ever noticed that when you mention Bible history everyone's eyes glaze over and a dull gray cloud settles over the room? Yet when when you mention the word *food* there is a distinct interest (particularly in children). How much more fun history would be if you could eat your way through it. That is the inspiration behind the Milk and Honey Cooking School.

Daphna Flegal and I were attending the Christian Educator's Fellowship in New Orleans, Louisiana [prior to Hurricane Katrina]—an area known for its excellent cuisine. As an "extra" to the conference we signed up for "The New Orleans Cooking School." We were expecting good food to eat and good recipes to take home and try out on our families. How surprised we were to find that and more.

Our chef not only prepared foods typical of Louisiana but also told the history of the area as she cooked. With each group of people that moved into the area, new foods, new seasonings, new preparation techniques followed as well. That's how the famous cuisine of the French Quarter came to be.

The light bulb flashed on! Why couldn't we teach the history of God's people using the same methods? We could talk about the culinary changes that occurred with every historical period and every army that marched through the little country of Palestine. So that's where the idea for the Milk and Honey Cooking School began.

We have combined Scripture references, historical data, cultural tidbits, and a little that we know of the hospitality of the lands of the Middle East to take you on a cooking and eating adventure. The Cooking School begins with Adam's first bite of the forbidden fruit and shows how foods, seasonings, and preparation methods changed as the Hebrew people came in contact with the outside world. We focus on the major historical periods—the Patriarchal Period (Abraham, Isaac, Jacob, and Joseph), the Egyptian Period (Joseph through Moses), the time of the Babylonian Exile, the Greek period, and the New Testament period into which Jesus was born.

This is more than a workshop or a Sunday school lesson. It is an event, because it takes a great deal of pre-planning. But it is an unforgettable experience for the presenters as well as the participants. Daphna and I have thoroughly enjoyed the times we have presented the cooking school and have had much positive feedback from those who participated. The school does require a little practice. We practiced on the children's team at the United Methodist Publishing House and a few invited guests. Everyone had a wonderful time and learned a great deal.

So join us on an eating and learning adventure. Tuck your napkin under your chin and off we go.

LeeDell Stickler

MILK and
HONEY
COOKING
SCHOOL

Overview

7

THE COOKING SCHOOL

The cooking school takes approximately 1.5 hours to present. The more people you have, the more time it will take. Let the people relax and enjoy the experience. Don't rush them.

Preparation Time

Allow one to four days to prepare. Many recipes can be done in advance, but half the fun is watching the presenters present and cook at the same time. For example, you can prepare one recipe of the Date Nut Halvah Balls ahead of time and refrigerate. Then prepare a second batch during the cooking school. Smaller batches are easier to do in a food processor anyway.

Number of Participants

To fully experience the table hospitality and rituals, there should be at least eight participants in the cooking school. Forty is ideal, but hectic.

Space

You will need a rather large space to present the cooking school. A fellowship hall or large social room provides the ideal setting.

Seating

You will need two sets of seating—tables and chairs that will accommodate everyone (eight people to a table), plus a second set of chairs around the perimeter of the room for the beginning of the cooking school. In Bible times, guests never went directly to the table where the food was to be served. They were "invited" to the table, and then took their places as their status determined. Participants will select a card (Page 62) from an envelope to determine who will be the host (H) and the ranking of the remainder of the table.

UNDERSTANDING THE CULTURE

The Milk and Honey Cooking School does more than just entertain and teach a little biblical history. It provides a more in-depth look at the culture of the Middle East. Most Westerners find the cooking and eating rituals of the Middle East a trifle odd (we who have mastered the TV trays in front of the television set). As we come to an understanding of the *what*s and the *how*s, we have a better feeling for the *why*s.

Because there were no knives, forks, or spoons used for eating, clean hands were a necessity. However, guests would never dip their hands in a basin of water. The guest would hold the hands over the basin while the servant or host poured clean water over them. The dirty water would collect in the basin, out of sight.

Tables could be as simple as the leather or cloth mat on the floor or the triclinium table used in New Testament times. The position for eating was usually sitting upright with legs folded under the body or reclining on mats or cushions. The only dishes used were those that contained the food.

Scripture mandated that grace be said at the beginning and the end of the meal. Frequently a guest was asked to give thanks and the rest of the diners would respond "Amen" at the end. After the meal washing the hands of course was essential and guests would dry their hands on a towel.

Think of the meals you have read about in the Bible, both Old and New Testament. Think about how each of the steps above was carried out in the text.

APPLIANCES

Food Processor

Several of the recipes can be prepared more quickly using a food processor. For example, make the Haroset a day ahead of time and store it in the refrigerator. Prepare one recipe of the Date Nut Halvah Balls prior to the event. Prepare a second recipe during the event so the participants can enjoy the preparation. (Expect people to ask for seconds of this one!)

Electric Skillet

The larger the better. The Roman Bread Pudding tastes great, and since it is toward the end of the meal, many persons will want more than just a nibble or taste.

Electric Griddle

Cooking the Unleavened Bread moves quickly. A large electric griddle makes it possible to keep adding new rounds of dough onto the surface as the cooked ones are removed. You will be making two batches of Unleavened Bread, so don't forget to double the recipe.

Crock Pot

This piece of equipment is particularly helpful in the preparation of Esau's Pottage. Start the ingredients the night before and let them cook all night. Or make the pottage on the stove and use the crock pot to keep it warm until time to serve.

GROCERY LIST

- ❏ feta cheese
- ❏ plain yogurt
- ❏ dill, parsley, mint
- ❏ walnuts
- ❏ whole wheat flour
- ❏ olive oil
- ❏ salt
- ❏ onion
- ❏ ground cumin and coriander
- ❏ garlic
- ❏ chicken stock
- ❏ red lentils
- ❏ spinach
- ❏ barley
- ❏ millet
- ❏ wheat kernels
- ❏ yeast
- ❏ sugar
- ❏ butter
- ❏ bread flour
- ❏ eggs
- ❏ poppy seeds
- ❏ almonds
- ❏ pitted dates
- ❏ dried apricots
- ❏ raisins
- ❏ cinnamon
- ❏ orange juice or lemon juice
- ❏ lemon zest; lemon rinds
- ❏ pine nuts
- ❏ ricotta cheese
- ❏ honey
- ❏ whole wheat pie crust
- ❏ milk
- ❏ ciabatta bread
- ❏ apples
- ❏ grape juice
- ❏ matzo crackers

BASIC STUFF

In addition to the groceries and the appliances, here are some things you will need.

❑ Provide a stole for the host at each table. Cut brightly colored fabric into six-inch by thirty-six-inch strips. Choose a fabric that does not unravel easily so you won't have to hem the stoles.

❑ Provide a pitcher, a large bowl, and a hand towel for each table. (Discounts stores are great for this.)

❑ Provide cloth napkins for the participants. (Borrow.)

❑ You will need hand sanitizers for each table. The participants will be eating with their hands, just as guests did in Bible times.

❑ Use paper bowls for the Roman Bread Pudding and Haroset. This will help with clean-up after the event.

❑ Provide a variety of baskets as serving dishes for the bread. Line each basket with a cloth napkin.

❑ For the grain-grinding experience, you will need two or three flat rocks and two or three round river rocks for each table. More than one set per table will give people more time to actually experience the process. Check with a local quarry.

❑ Provide a variety of small resealable containers for pre-measuring spices, olive oil, and other ingredients.

PERSONNEL

Presenters/Cooks: You will need two. While one is talking, the other will be doing the cooking. Select persons who can work well together and who have a good sense of humor. The timing on this event is crucial. But no matter how hard you plan, something always goes wrong. Laugh about it. So will the audience.

Greeter: This person will meet the participants at the door and direct them to the seats around the perimeter of the room. The greeter will also be the one to remove the napkin from the door as was the custom. (As long as the napkin was on the door, guests could be seated. When the napkin was removed, then the dinner had begun and no one else was allowed to come in.)

Servers: You will need at least one server for each two tables. If you limit the number of participants to no more than forty, that is approximately five tables. You will need at least three servers. The server will receive the cooked food from the cooking station and deliver it to the tables or will take the pre-prepared food from the serving center to the tables. Servers will also be responsible for cleaning up any accidents that occur.

Grocery Shopper: If you have someone who actually enjoys tracking down unusual foods, this is a particularly good assignment for them. Most of the foods are familiar. Check the number of servings with each recipe. Purchase enough of each item to accommodate your workshop.

Baker: Invite someone who truly loves to bake to make the Challah Braid ahead of time. This bread freezes well.

GOING INTERGENERATIONAL

The Milk and Honey Cooking School is one of those events that can be enjoyed by persons of a variety of age levels.

Except for the actual cooking, which involves sharp instruments and hot appliances, there is no other job in the event that cannot be done by either an adult or a child. The only limitation might be interest.

Elementary children will certainly be interested in the different foods and the activities surrounding the cooking and eating. They may or may not be able to follow all the historical data.

An elementary child can participate in all levels of this event, including being a host at one of the tables, should he or she draw the "H" card. The weight of the water pitcher may be the only drawback for this role. An adult at the table can assist. The event lasts for approximately one and a half hours. There is some moving around, but most of the event requires sitting at the table. Pre-schoolers would have a difficult time maintaining interest between the courses.

Youth and older elementary boys and girls can be servers.

Make sure the participants at each table are mixed. You don't want a table of all children or all adults. The participants will learn from one another as they sample and experience the variety of activities.

PLANNING AHEAD

Planning ahead is the secret to success for this particular event. You don't want to prepare all of the foods ahead of time. That would spoil the fun. Nevertheless, you can pre-measure most of the dry ingredients as well as divide up the grains into small cups with lids. Then just store them until the day of the event.

The week before

❏ Prepare loaves of Challah Braid (See page 58). Freeze. This particular bread freezes well. Make sure it is wrapped tightly to seal in the flavor.

❏ Prepare the signs for the various periods: Patriarchal Period, Egyptian Period, Babylonian Period, Greek Period, New Testament (Roman) Period.

❏ Photocopy the Table Hierarchy Cards (page 62). Cut them apart and put each set in an envelope. You will need one envelope for each table of eight.

❏ Photocopy the Scriptures (pages 49–54). Cut them apart. Store in an envelope until the day of the event.

❏ Cut a stole (See page 12) for the host of each table.

❏ Purchase groceries for the event. If you are dividing the food preparation, make sure each "cook" has the supplies he or she needs.

The Day Before

❑ Prepare Honey Cheesecake (See page 60). Chill. (Option: Purchase prepared cheesecake bites.)

❑ Prepare the Haroset (See page 61) and refrigerate.

❑ Remove Challah Braid (See page 58) from the freezer to defrost.

❑ Measure ingredients for the Goat Cheese Dip (See page 56) and put into small sealed containers. You will need one set of containers for each table. Refrigerate.

❑ Measure the dry ingredients for the Unleavened Bread. Store in sealed containers so that the cooks can simply "dump" each container into the mixing bowl.

❑ Prepare one recipe of the Date Nut Halvah Balls (See page 59). Store in a sealed container and refrigerate.

❑ Measure a set of the ingredients for the Date Nut Halvah Balls (See page 59) that you plan to prepare during the workshop. Store each ingredient in a separate sealed container.

❑ Cut ciabatta bread for Roman Bread Pudding (See page 61) into cubes and store in a sealed container.

❑ Make a copy of the Menu (page 63) for each participant.

❑ Set up the chairs and the eating tables. (See Room Arrangement, pages 19–20.)

❑ Test the appliances to make sure that each of them actually works.

Two to Three Hours Before

❏ Set out the thirteen Bible Scriptures. Divide them evenly among the tables for individual guests to read when prompted.

❏ Fill pitchers with water. (You will need one pitcher for each table.) Place them on the tables. (See Table Setting Arrangement, pages 21–22.)

❏ Place bowls, towels, and hand sanitizer on each table.

❏ Set up the two serving stations on opposite sides of the room. (See Serving Center Arrangement, pages 25–26.)

❏ Set up the cooking station. (See Cooking Station Arrangement, pages 23–24.)

❏ Test the appliances in place on the cooking station with all devices on at the same time. If you must throw a circuit breaker, do it now before the event begins.

❏ Set out the envelope(s) with the seating cards inside.

❏ If you are using purchased cheesecake bites rather than Honey Cheesecake (See page 60), allow them to begin defrosting now.

❏ Assign servers to their tables.

❏ Place a dinner napkin over the doorknob of the main entry door into the workshop space. If you have two main entrances, place napkins on both doors.

Fifteen to Thirty Minutes Before

❏ Place containers of feta cheese and yogurt on the tables.

❏ Place containers with barley, wheat, and millet on the tables.

❏ Place cloth napkins in each basket.

❏ Break two loaves of the Challah Braid into smaller bites. Keep one loaf intact to show the "breaking of the bread."

❏ Divide the Haroset into the serving bowls (one for each table) and place on the serving table out of the way.

❏ Place a copy of the Menu for the meal (See page 63) in each chair around the perimeter of the room.

❏ Position the greeter at the door to guide participants as they come into the room.

❏ Pour the milk over the ciabatta bread for the Roman Bread Pudding. Stir. Set aside.

❏ The two presenters/cooks should put on their aprons and take their places at the cooking station.

SETTING UP
FOR THE
COOKING SCHOOL

Room Arrangement Checklist

❏ Arrange the tables so that no one has his or her back to
the cooking station (if possible)—even if you are using
round tables. There should be eight chairs at each eating
table.

❏ Leave walking room between tables for the servers so
that they can move freely without having to ask
participants to "scoot in."

❏ Make sure the cooking station has plenty of elbow room.
Use two tables if necessary. When things get moving,
you don't have time to be polite.

❏ Line up chairs around the perimeter of the room. There
should be a chair for each participant. Do not allow
guests to come to the tables until they are invited.

Room Arrangement

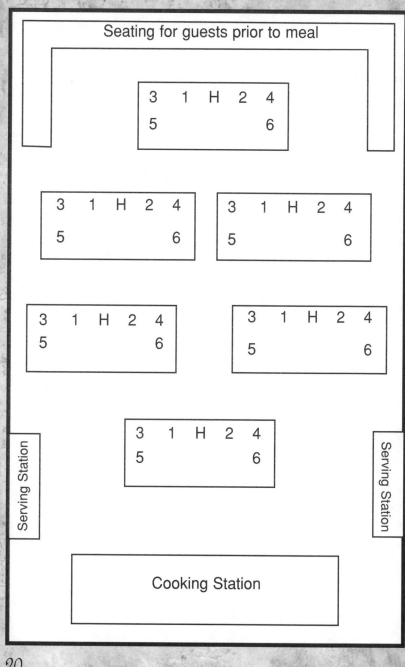

Seating for guests prior to meal

| 3 | 1 | H | 2 | 4 |
| 5 | | | | 6 |

| 3 | 1 | H | 2 | 4 |
| 5 | | | | 6 |

| 3 | 1 | H | 2 | 4 |
| 5 | | | | 6 |

| 3 | 1 | H | 2 | 4 |
| 5 | | | | 6 |

| 3 | 1 | H | 2 | 4 |
| 5 | | | | 6 |

| 3 | 1 | H | 2 | 4 |
| 5 | | | | 6 |

Serving Station

Serving Station

Cooking Station

Table Setting Checklist

Each table will need the following items:

- ❏ a cloth stole for the host of the table
- ❏ a tablecloth
- ❏ a pitcher of water, a large bowl, a towel
- ❏ a flat rock, a grinding stone
- ❏ three small cups with grain (barley, millet, wheat)
- ❏ pre-measured mint, parsley, dill, feta cheese, yogurt, empty bowl, plastic spoon
- ❏ hand sanitizer, cloth napkins
- ❏ a dispenser for the honey (small bowl or squeeze bottle)

Helpful Hint: Put a distinguishing mark on the containers to be used for grinding grain. Or use containers distinctly different from those used for the goat cheese dip. In one of our workshops, we had one table combine the barley and millet with the goat cheese. It made for an interesting spread for the unleavened bread. (A little too crunchy for us.)

Table Setting Arrangement

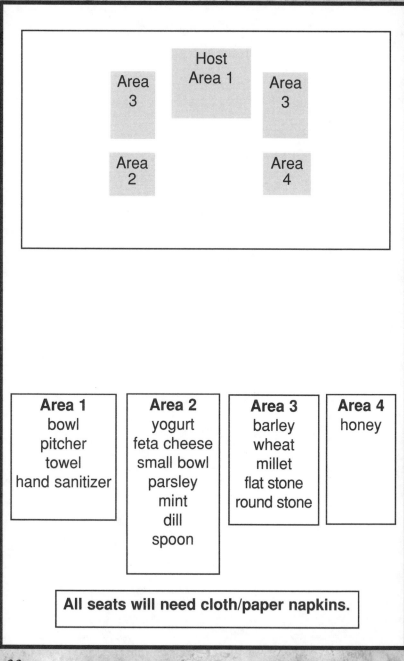

Host
Area 1

Area 3

Area 3

Area 2

Area 4

Area 1
bowl
pitcher
towel
hand sanitizer

Area 2
yogurt
feta cheese
small bowl
parsley
mint
dill
spoon

Area 3
barley
wheat
millet
flat stone
round stone

Area 4
honey

All seats will need cloth/paper napkins.

Cooking Station Checklist

Give yourself plenty of room at the cooking station. If you have room for two tables, use them. You won't regret it. Provide easels or document holders for the scripts. Don't rely on your memory. Many of the recipes require timing to have them ready when you reach that section of the script.

You will need the following at the cooking station:

- ❏ an electric griddle, spatula (Unleavened Bread)
- ❏ an electric skillet, spoon (Roman Bread Pudding)
- ❏ a food processor, knife, scraper (Date Nut Halvah Balls)
- ❏ a crock pot, large serving spoon (Esau's Pottage)
- ❏ measuring spoons
- ❏ two bowls of water and a towel (clean-up)
- ❏ large mixing bowl, large mixing spoon, fork, salt, premeasured containers of whole wheat flour, olive oil, and water (Unleavened Bread)
- ❏ pre-measured containers of walnuts, dates, apricots, raisins, orange or lemon juice, cinnamon, lemon zest (Date Nut Halvah Balls)
- ❏ olive oil, bread cubes, milk, honey (Roman Bread Pudding)

Cooking Station Arrangement

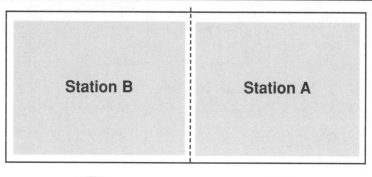

 cook

 cook

Station B
(Leader 2)
script
food processor
knife
scraper
crock pot
large serving spoon
bowl of water
towel
pre-measured containers
  of walnuts, dates,
  apricots, raisins, orange
  juice, cinnamon, lemon
  zest
Challah Braid

Station A
(Leader 1)
script
electric griddle
spatula
electric skillet
spoon
container of bread cubes
pre-measured containers
  of whole wheat flour,
  olive oil, water
measuring spoons
olive oil (bread pudding)
milk (bread pudding)
bowl of water
towel

Serving Center Checklist

The serving centers will be the second most active area in this event. Provide two centers, one on either side of the room. This prevents servers from having to cross in front of the presenters or perhaps bump into one another. You will need one server for each two tables if possible.

For each serving center you will need:

- ❑ a basket for each table's Unleavened Bread
- ❑ a large Pottage serving bowl for each table
- ❑ a stole for the host of the table
- ❑ a stack of bowls for the Roman Bread Pudding, one for each participant
- ❑ a tray for the Date Nut Halvah Balls
- ❑ plastic forks, one for each participant (Roman Bread Pudding)
- ❑ a tray of Honey Cheesecake or thawed cheesecake bites
- ❑ a basket with the Challah Braid
- ❑ a bowl of Haroset for each table
- ❑ a bowl of matzo crackers for each table
- ❑ towels and a bowl of water for clean-up

Serving Center Arrangement

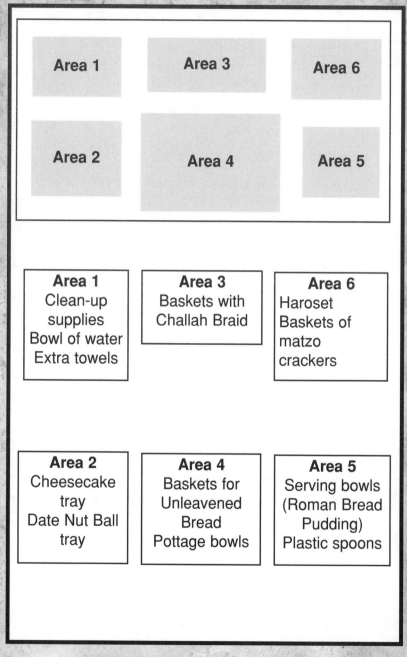

Area 1 Clean-up supplies Bowl of water Extra towels	**Area 3** Baskets with Challah Braid	**Area 6** Haroset Baskets of matzo crackers
Area 2 Cheesecake tray Date Nut Ball tray	**Area 4** Baskets for Unleavened Bread Pottage bowls	**Area 5** Serving bowls (Roman Bread Pudding) Plastic spoons

MILK and
HONEY
COOKING
SCHOOL

Script

27

Greeter instructs persons as they enter to take a seat around the perimeter of the room and not at the tables. Menus will be on the perimeter chairs.

Leader 1:

Welcome to the Milk and Honey Cooking School. Today we invite you to enter the world of the Bible in an unusual way—through the kitchen door, or at least their version of the kitchen door.

Did you know that Bible history virtually begins with an act of eating? *(Invite the person who finds Scripture #1 at his or her seat to stand and read it aloud; do the same with each Scripture as you come to it.)*

Scripture #1

The woman stared at the fruit. It looked beautiful and tasty. She wanted the wisdom that it would give her, and she ate some of the fruit. Her husband was there with her, so she gave some to him, and he ate it too. (Genesis 3:6)

Leader 2:

And from that point on food continues to play an important role in the life of the people of the Bible.

The cuisine of the Bible was a healthful one. All bread and grain were of the whole-grain variety. Vegetarian and dairy meals were popular. Beans, grains, and raw vegetables were eaten frequently, as well as yogurt and cheese. Poultry and fish were served more often than meat. Fruits and nuts were ingredients and sauces, and refined sugar didn't even exist.

28

Leader 1:

Cooking and eating carried with them certain rituals. We intend to help you experience some of these rituals as we also experience some of the foods of the Bible.

 Invite the people to come to the tables, where they will each draw a card from the Table Hierarchy envelope. The participant who draws the "H" becomes the host and places the stole around his or her shoulders. The others will seat themselves around the table in order of their "importance." The host will take the center seat. Then the remaining participants at the table will arrange themselves accordingly. The most important person (1) will be seated to the right of the host. The second most important person (2) will be seated on the left. Then they will alternate, right and left, moving farther from the host, until everyone is seated.

 Instruct the host of the table to "wash" everyone's hands. Each guest will hold his or her hands over the large bowl and the host will pour water from the pitcher over the guest's hands. Then the host will wipe the guest's hands with the towel.

As long as the napkins were draped over the door, the guests might continue to enter. Once the napkins were removed, no more guests were permitted and the meal could begin. (*Remove the napkin[s] from the door[s].*)

Palestine's location alone made it a natural candidate for culinary assimilation. This small country served as a land bridge between some of history's most powerful armies. As the armies marched through the land, the foods they ate were brought along with them. We will begin with the culinary fare of the nomadic tribes, represented by Abraham and Sarah and their descendants, and end with one of the most famous meals of all—The Last Supper of Jesus and his disciples.

So tuck your napkin under your chin and get your taste buds ready. Here we go!

Blessing of the Food:

Blessed art Thou, Jehovah our God, King of the world, who causes to come forth bread from the earth. Amen.

 Begin cooking the Unleavened Bread.

PATRIARCHAL PERIOD

Leader 2:

Life for Abraham and Sarah was largely nomadic. They were the herdsmen of the desert. They raised sheep, goats, and camels. They lived their simple lives in the midst of this barrenness. Even their housing was simple—tents woven from the hair of their goats that could be taken down and moved as they searched for food for their flocks. The word for "table" literally meant a piece of leather or a mat on the floor.

These families hunted wild birds, milked and managed their flocks, gathered herbs to season their food, and tended semi-wild crops of barley, figs, and grapes. Their diet consisted of savory stews, roasted lamb, grilled quail, fresh curd cheese, macerated fruit, unleavened breads, and parched grain salads. And hospitality, rather than being a rarity, was expected.

Scripture #2

One hot summer afternoon Abraham was sitting by the entrance to his tent near the sacred trees of Mamre, when the Lord appeared to him. Abraham looked up and saw three men standing nearby. He quickly ran to meet them, bowed with his face to the ground, and said, "Please come to my home where I can serve you. I'll have some water brought, so you can wash your feet. Then you can rest under the tree. Let me get you some food to give you strength before you leave. I would be honored to serve you." "Thank you very much," they answered. "We accept your offer." Abraham quickly went to his tent and said to Sarah, "Hurry! Get a large sack of flour and make some bread." After saying this, he rushed off to his herd of cattle and picked out one of the best calves, which his servant quickly prepared. He then served his guests some yogurt and milk together with the meat. (Genesis 18:1–8)

Abraham was the consummate host. But then, any desert family of this period would have done the same. Guests in the home were assumed to be sent from God, and it was the family's sacred duty to make them feel welcome. Perfect strangers were welcomed as if they were long-lost friends. Besides, the arrival of a stranger was a rare and welcome occasion—a good chance to keep up with the news of the outside world.

When a guest came into a home, the host bowed to the ground in welcome. Then he greeted each guest with a kiss, placing the right hand on the left shoulder of the guest and kissing the right cheek. Then the action was reversed, placing the left hand on the right shoulder and kissing the left cheek. *(Demonstrate.)*

 Have the host practice this with the persons seated at her or his table. Allow several minutes for this activity.

Abraham offered to the strangers who came that day the very best that he had. Such hospitality was important to these desert dwellers. To show kindness to a guest was to honor one's God, and in turn God would show kindness to the family. As Abraham did that hot day, you are going to prepare a simple appetizer of goat cheese and yogurt to serve on the Unleavened Bread.

 Invite the host at the table to prepare the goat cheese dip by combining the cups of feta cheese, yogurt, parsley, dill, and mint in the bowls provided. Pass out the first round of Unleavened Bread for the people to dip into the cheese and taste.

You might think that the women only prepared the foods and never knew what was going on. It is true that the tents of the nomads were divided into two sections, one for the men and one for the women. The sections were separated by a curtain. The men's area opened with an awning to the sun. Here the men would welcome guests and entertain them. The women's section was strictly off limits to any man but the head of the household. Here would have been all the household supplies, the clothing, and the cooking utensils. But this didn't mean that the women were left out. They could peek through the curtains and eavesdrop on any conversation. Imagine her surprise when Sarah was "caught" red-handed listening at the tent divider.

Scripture #3

While they were eating, he stood near them under the trees, and they asked, "Where is your wife Sarah?" "She is right there in the tent," Abraham answered. One of the guests was the Lord, and he said, "I'll come back about this time next year, and when I do, Sarah will already have a son." Sarah was behind Abraham, listening at the entrance to the tent. Abraham and Sarah were very old, and Sarah was well past the age for having children. So she laughed and said to herself, "Now that I am worn out and my husband is old, will I really know such happiness?" (Genesis 18:8b–12)

Little did Abraham know that he was entertaining such heavenly guests.

Leader 1:

As God promised, Abraham did indeed become the father of a great nation. Isaac was born. When Isaac grew up, he married Rebekah, and they had the twins Jacob and Esau, whom I'm sure you have heard about. So we invite you to sample another common dish of the time—the pottage that Jacob served to his brother Esau. This is probably one of the most famous recipes in the history of the Bible. The story goes that Esau, the elder of the twins, comes home from an extended hunting trip. His brother Jacob has prepared a savory lentil stew. The smell of the stew is more than Esau's hungry stomach can take. So very imprudently, Esau gives his birthright in exchange for a bowl of that "red stuff."

The stew was a vegetarian variety, as meat was hard to

come by. Obviously Esau was a good hunter and provided meat for the stews that his father liked. Meat spoiled quickly, and since drying was the only means of preservation they had, it was limited. Besides, meat usually meant diminishing the herds and was only used on special occasions.

Scripture #4

As Jacob and Esau grew older, Esau liked the outdoors and became a good hunter, while Jacob settled down and became a shepherd. Esau would take the meat of wild animals to his father Isaac, and so Isaac loved him more, but Jacob was his mother's favorite son. One day, Jacob was cooking some stew, when Esau came home hungry and said, "I'm starving to death! Give me some of that red stew right now!" That's how Esau got the name "Edom." Jacob replied, "Sell me your rights as the first-born son." "I'm about to die," Esau answered. "What good will those rights do me?" But Jacob said, "Promise me your birthrights, here and now!" And that's what Esau did. Jacob then gave Esau some bread and some of the bean stew, and when Esau had finished eating and drinking, he just got up and left, showing how little he thought of his rights as the first born. (Genesis 25:27–34)

You know the rest of the story, which brings us to the next move that took the people of God into the land of Egypt and a whole new culinary experience.

 Have the servers bring a bowl of Esau's Pottage to each of the tables. Instruct the people on the etiquette of eating with the Unleavened Bread.

Demonstrate how to break off a piece of the bread and use it as a scoop for the pottage. Serve the second round of Unleavened Bread. Remind the people that "double dipping" was just as impolite in Bible times as it is today. Also, the right hand was the only one used for eating, as the left hand was used for hygienic purposes. Give the people time to enjoy the biblical eating experience.

EGYPTIAN PERIOD

Leader 1:

From the time of Joseph until the Exodus, the Hebrews learned much during their sojourn in Egypt. Advances in kitchen arts flourished as well as the art of baking and brewing. Not to mention pottery. The invention of pottery brought about one of the most valuable tools of primitive times. Archaeologists notice that a change in culture often coincided with a change in pottery.

 If you have several examples of hand-thrown and fired pottery, set these out for people to look at. Instruct them to look at the form of the pot, the opening of the pot, and the handles if there are any.

In Egypt, grain took on a whole new dimension. Grain has long been humanity's basic form of nourishment. What we know today is that it is the perfect vegetable food source. The cultivation of grain is considered the beginning of civilization. And beginning grain cultivation requires new technology—plows to turn the ground, hoes to remove the weeds, pottery to store the grain, millstones to grind it into flour.

Growing grain also meant a stationary existence. As the people began a period of cultivating food, communities became more stable. There was no longer a need to move around. But there was soon another important discovery. With all its advantages, people quickly learned that grain could not be easily digested in its raw form. It had to be cooked. That's when the fun began.

Scripture #5

Joseph was thirty when the king made him governor, and he went everywhere for the king. For seven years there were big harvests of grain. Joseph collected and stored up the extra grain in the cities of Egypt near the fields where it was harvested. In fact, there was so much grain that they stopped keeping record, because it was like counting the grains of sand along the beach. (Genesis 41:46–49)

With the abundance of grain in Egypt, the people soon discovered that grain could be sprouted, pounded, dried, crushed, reconstituted, and fermented. (For those of you who might not know, fermented grain produces a kind of beer.) Grains were served at every meal in some form or another—green, boiled, parched, soaked and roasted, baked into puddings, flans, and casseroles. (Somehow I always thought the casserole was the invention of the twentieth-century working wife.)

Grain was common. Bread, on the other hand, was a luxury. Why? Because it took hours of pounding, grinding, and sifting to make the flour that was needed to make bread.

Before you on the table are three of the main varieties of grain found in Egypt—millet, barley, and wheat. Take some time to get familiar with them. Using the rocks provided on your table, pound them into a semblance of flour.

 Give the participants time to inspect the various grains in the cups on the table. Then have each table sprinkle a few grains onto the flat rock and use the round rock to "grind" the grain into flour. Allow several minutes for the people to create a little "flour" on their stones.

Do you have more respect for the women of the Bible who did this? Remember, some people are doing this still. What do you find in your flour with the wheat or the barley? *(stone)* The people of Bible times found this too, and for this reason their teeth were often worn down as they aged from eating the ground stone.

Of the three main grains there were advantages and disadvantages of each.

- Millet cannot produce yeast, but it cooked in twenty to forty minutes.

- Barley took an hour to cook, but it was the most plentiful grain and the chief producer of flour.

- Barley produced more grain per acre than wheat and required less water for cultivation. But barley also lacked gluten, which was the protein that made yeast.

- Wheat, on the other hand, was the most complete grain. It produced yeast, but it also took four to six hours to cook. So not only was it extravagant in the use of time, but it was also extravagant in the use of firewood.

- A particular plus in favor of wheat, however, was that the yearly flooding of the Nile allowed for its cultivation.

Leader 2:

The unleavened bread that the Hebrew people were used to was a flat bread, similar to a tortilla. When it was cool, it became like a dry cracker or crisp bread. It was used as an eating utensil, dipped into the bowl where the stew was served.

The introduction of yeast for bread created a whole new level of bread making. But the Hebrews didn't always trust the process of leavening. Lightness was trickery while heaviness was considered wholesome and natural. But they soon became accustomed to the fare that they had, even as slaves in Egypt.

Scripture #6

In Egypt we could eat all the fish we wanted, and there were cucumbers, melons, onions, and garlic. But we're starving out here, and the only food we have is the manna. (Numbers 11:5–6)

Did you know that ancient writings have uncovered over thirty different varieties of yeast breads in Egypt prior to the Exodus? We invite you to sample one of them. It's called Challah Braid, and the Hebrew people soon adopted this bread into their religious festivities. You've experienced the Unleavened Bread, now experience the lightness of bread that has risen.

 Serve the Challah Braid. Give the servers time to pass the bread before going on.

When the time came for God's people to leave the land of Egypt, they did so with great drama. We have heard the story of how the angel of death passed over the homes of the Hebrew people where the blood of the lamb was obvious. They were told to leave, and to leave in such a hurry that their bread didn't even have time to rise.

Once in the land that God promised to them, the people of God built their own unique national culinary identity. Some of their uniqueness was based on foods that were consumed (or not consumed) and the ways these foods were prepared. For example, it was during this period that the rule was developed that forbade the consumption of young goat meat that had been boiled in its mother's milk.

Scripture #7

You may eat any animal that has divided hoofs and chews the cud. But you must not eat animals such as camels, rock badgers, and rabbits that chew the cud but don't have divided hoofs. And you must not eat pigs—they have divided hoofs, but don't chew the cud. All of these animals are unclean, and you are forbidden even to touch their dead bodies. You may eat anything that lives in water and has fins and scales. But it would be disgusting for you to eat anything else that lives in the water, and you must not even touch their dead bodies.

(Leviticus 11:2–12)

 Begin cooking the Roman Bread Pudding at this point. Stir frequently to keep it from overbrowning.

THE BABYLONIAN PERIOD

Leader 1:

And the list went on and on and on.

For hundreds of years God's people dwelled in the land of milk and honey. Then came a momentous event, which, although devastating for the people of Israel, made a significant impact on their lives, including the food they ate. The Israelites were conquered by the Babylonians. Many inhabitants of Israel were forced into exile in Babylon. This was a shrewd move on the part of the Babylonians, as it removed the important political figures from the land, thus preventing them from reorganizing and being a constant source of trouble for the foreign army. But what this also did was introduce to the Hebrew people a brand new cuisine.

 Begin to prepare the second batch of Date Nut Halvah Balls. To add a little humor, as the Leader begins to talk, start the food processor. Do this several times, forcing the Leader to wait until the fruits have been processed.

All of a sudden the Hebrew people who had been forced from their lands were being exposed to a land that was rich in culinary history. It was a land of luscious fruits, including cherries, peaches, plums, and apples. Walnuts and pistachios were particularly common. This cuisine was known throughout the ancient world for its delicate spicing and rich sauces.

The Hebrew people naturally were influenced by this change in culture. The Babylonians treated the exiles well. They could meet freely, buy property, and practice their own customs and religion. Even though they adopted some of the culture (for example, the Aramaic language, the alphabet, and the calendar), they did try to retain their national identity by attaching special importance to some of their practices, particularly the dietary laws. (*Serve the Date Nut Halvah Balls.*)

Scripture #8

> Daniel made up his mind to eat and drink only what God had approved for his people to eat. And he asked the king's chief official for permission not to eat the food and wine served in the royal palace. (Daniel 1:8)

When Cyrus of Persia conquered Babylon, the long Jewish exile came to an end. The people were free to return to Jerusalem—however, at first, very few did. Cyrus united all the Persian tribes into one great nation. When Xerxes succeeded his father Darius to the throne of Persia, he inherited a vast and well-organized empire. The empire was held together by organization and discipline and did not fall until the time of Alexander the Great. Roads were well maintained, which promoted trade among the various parts of the nation, which extended from Greece in the west to India in the east.

New foods and cooking styles were introduced. Archaeologists have actually found cooking records and detailed accounts of lavish banquets from this period of history. For example, the Book of Esther begins with a banquet that lasted for 180 days. That's three months. (I thought Benjamin Franklin's three-day guest rule was being more than generous.)

Scripture #9

> During the third year of his rule, Xerxes gave a big dinner for all his officials and officers. The governors and leaders of the provinces were also invited, and even the commanders of the Persian and Median armies came. For one hundred eighty days he showed off his wealth and spent a lot of money to impress his guests with the greatness of his kingdom.
>
> (Esther 1:3–4)

THE GREEK PERIOD

Leader 2:

For more than one hundred years the people of Palestine lived under Persian rule. At this time a young man named Alexander inherited a war that his father Philip of Macedon began. Now, Philip's intention was only to conquer Asia Minor, but Alexander's aim became the total destruction of the Persian Empire. For the Jews of Palestine, they were now a part of the Greek-speaking world. It marked not only a major historical turning point, but a culinary turning point as well.

The Greeks, and the Hellenists who copied them, were sophisticated diners. Their meals followed a definite set of courses. They served hors d'oeuvres before the meal, then the entree, which was followed by a dessert, then more drinking of wine with lively philosophical conversation. The Jews began serving roasted giblets of paschal lambs on beds of lettuce leaves as the hors d'oeuvres of the Passover supper. The Babylonian custom of dipping greens into salt water and herbal vinegar remained, but now it was the giblets in lettuce leaves that were dipped.

The Greeks also introduced advanced methods into the production of wine. They even created a superior vessel for this purpose—the amphora. These were used by the Greeks for the storage and shipping of wines and oils. But improved methods of wine production also increased the opportunity for drunkenness. This scandalized the religious Jews, and they began to add water, not just to smooth the taste, but to forestall drunkenness altogether. They made adding water to wine mandatory. But still, since the Greek period wine has been an obligation and an important part of the celebration of Passover.

Scripture #10

At the feast there were six stone water jars that were used by the people for washing themselves in the way that their religion said they must. Each jar held about twenty or thirty gallons. Jesus told the servants to fill them to the top with water. Then after the jars had been filled, he said, "Now take some water and give it to the man in charge of the feast." The servants did as Jesus told them, and the man in charge drank some of the water that had now turned into wine. He did not know where the wine had come from, but the servants did. He

called the bridegroom over and said, "The best wine is always served first. Then after the guests have had plenty, the other wine is served. But you have kept the best until last!"
(John 2:6–10)

Leader 1:

In dietary matters, the Greeks were concerned with health, exercise, and balance. How much one ate, in what combination of foods, and at what time of day were as important as the specific menu. They were fond of shrimp, rabbit, herbed broths, flax breads, black puddings, and cheesecake. (Who isn't fond of cheesecake?)

 Serve the Honey Cheesecake (or cheesecake bites).

Thousands of Greek settlers swarmed into Samaria and Galilee, mingling with the already diverse population. The Greeks were tireless city-builders and founded urban centers based on the Greek model all along the Mediterranean area, in lower Galilee, and in the desert beyond the Jordan River. All of these settlements took on Hellenistic characteristics and attracted forward-thinking Jewish citizens.

NEW TESTAMENT PERIOD

Leader 2:

The Greek empire eventually fell to the might of Rome. Roman rule would be strict and increasingly oppressive. The dream of a Messiah became a national pastime. But in spite of Roman oppression, Jewish culture flourished.

The extravagance of the Roman banquet table is legendary. For example, an impressive appetizer of peacock tongues might require the demise of two hundred birds. In fact, laws were passed limiting the extravagance of banquets, but as you might expect, enforcement of this proved difficult.

 Begin to serve the Roman Bread Pudding. Have the servers ready with trays or baskets to take more than one bowl at a time.

Scripture #11

About that time Emperor Augustus gave orders for the names of all the people to be listed in record books. These first records were made when Quirinius was governor of Syria. Everyone had to go to their own hometown to be listed. So Joseph had to leave Nazareth in Galilee and go to Bethlehem in Judea. Long ago Bethlehem had been King David's hometown, and Joseph went there because he was from David's family. Mary was engaged to Joseph and traveled with him to Bethlehem. She was soon going to have a baby, and

> while they were there, she gave birth to her first-born son.
> She dressed him in baby clothes and laid him on a bed of hay,
> because there was no room for them in the inn. (Luke 2:1–7)

Jesus was born into a world at peace—a Roman peace. As long as the Hebrew people kept out of trouble and paid their taxes, they were pretty much left alone to do whatever they wanted to do. It was a peace that was maintained by an extensive and well-trained Roman army. For the most part this peace brought prosperity and even a measure of luxury for the far-flung provinces. This was not true, however, for Palestine. The people there were little more than taxpaying units. But the straight roads and the soaring aqueducts that brought water down from the mountains provided an opportunity for another growth in culinary fare.

Jerusalem had been growing at a phenomenal rate ever since it had become a part of the Greek empire. At least three times a year Jerusalem hosted the pilgrims who came to worship in the Temple on the feasts of Passover, Pentecost, and Tabernacles. As the number of pilgrims grew to the millions, Jerusalem had to adjust. When it was no longer possible to accommodate everyone in the Temple courts for the Passover supper, the authorities separated the supper from the two Passover sacrifices. Soon Jerusalem was no longer able to provide housing for all the pilgrims. Villages within two miles of the city were annexed to house the pilgrims. Later, people were allowed to put their tents up in nearby open fields and hillsides. By the time of Jesus the crowds were so enormous that authorities granted special permission to use various rooftops and courtyards of all the buildings as "dining rooms."

Scripture #12

They asked him, "Where do you want us to make preparations for it?" "Listen," he said to them, "when you have entered the city, a man carrying a jar of water will meet you; follow him into the house he enters and say to the owner of the house, 'The teacher asks you, "Where is the guest room, where I may eat the Passover with my disciples?" ' He will show you a large room upstairs, already furnished. Make preparations for us there." (Luke 22:9–12, NRSV)

Before the meal, many preparations would have to be made. One of the most important was the removal of all leavening from the house. Even the scoops and the feathers used to collect the crumbs were burned in a fire in the courtyard. The dishes received a special purification ritual. To ensure purity, in the wealthier families, a separate set of dishes was kept strictly for the Passover meal. Large fires were built in the courtyards and a large cauldron of water was put on to boil. All the pots and pans and serving dishes and utensils were placed in this boiling water until they were purified.

We invite you to taste two of the more traditional dishes served at the Passover table. The matzo crackers reminded the people of the bread dough that did not have time to rise. The Haroset reminded the people of the mortar the slaves used to make the bricks.

 Invite the people to take a small portion of the matzo cracker and dip it into the Haroset for a taste. The matzo was often called the Afrikonen.

By Jesus' day tables were of various shapes. But the most common was known as a triclinium, or a three-sided table. It was about the height of today's coffee table and surrounded by low couches, common in the Roman world. The tables were often made of wood or stone. There was a base and the dining surface. After a meal, the entire surface piece would be taken outside and "shaken" to remove food particles.

One of the most famous of the New Testament references talks about the reclining at the table.

Scripture #13

After saying this Jesus was troubled in spirit, and declared, "Very truly, I tell you, one of you will betray me." The disciples looked at one another, uncertain of whom he was speaking. One of his disciples—the one whom Jesus loved— was reclining next to him; Simon Peter therefore motioned to him to ask Jesus of whom he was speaking. (John 13:21–24, NRSV)

Closing Blessing:

We give you thanks, O Lord, for the land you have given us which has brought forth the food that we have just eaten. Amen.

Invite the guests to remove the tablecloths from the table and shake the crumbs out.

SCRIPTURE PAGES

Scripture #1

The woman stared at the fruit. It looked beautiful and tasty. She wanted the wisdom that it would give her, and she ate some of the fruit. Her husband was there with her, so she gave some to him, and he ate it too.

(Genesis 3:6)

Scripture #2

One hot summer afternoon Abraham was sitting by the entrance to his tent near the sacred trees of Mamre, when the Lord appeared to him. Abraham looked up and saw three men standing nearby. He quickly ran to meet them, bowed with his face to the ground, and said, "Please come to my home where I can serve you. I'll have some water brought, so you can wash your feet, then you can rest under the tree. Let me get you some food to give you strength before you leave. I would be honored to serve you."

"Thank you very much," they answered. "We accept your offer."

Abraham quickly went to his tent and said to Sarah, "Hurry! Get a large sack of flour and make some bread." After saying this, he rushed off to his herd of cattle and picked out one of the best calves, which his servant quickly prepared. He then served his guests some yogurt and milk together with the meat.

(Genesis 18:1–8)

Scripture #3

While they were eating, he stood near them under the trees, and they asked, "Where is your wife Sarah?" "She is right there in the tent," Abraham answered. One of the guests was the Lord, and he said, "I'll come back about this time next year, and when I do, Sarah will already have a son."

Sarah was behind Abraham, listening at the entrance to the tent. Abraham and Sarah were very old, and Sarah was well past the age for having children. So she laughed and said to herself, "Now that I am worn out and my husband is old, will I really know such happiness?" (Genesis 18:8b–12)

Scripture #4

As Jacob and Esau grew older, Esau liked the outdoors and became a good hunter, while Jacob settled down and became a shepherd. Esau would take the meat of wild animals to his father Isaac, and so Isaac loved him more, but Jacob was his mother's favorite son.

One day, Jacob was cooking some stew, when Esau came home hungry and said, "I'm starving to death! Give me some of that red stew right now!" That's how Esau got the name "Edom."

Jacob replied, "Sell me your rights as the first-born son."

"I'm about to die," Esau answered. "What good will those rights do me?"

But Jacob said, "Promise me your birthrights, here and now!" And that's what Esau did. Jacob then gave Esau some bread and some of the bean stew, and when Esau had finished eating and drinking, he just got up and left, showing how little he thought of his rights as the first-born. (Genesis 25:27–34)

Scripture #5

Joseph was thirty when the king made him governor, and he went everywhere for the king. For seven years there were big harvests of grain. Joseph collected and stored up the extra grain in the cities of Egypt near the fields where it was harvested. In fact, there was so much grain that they stopped keeping record, because it was like counting the grains of sand along the beach.

(Genesis 41:46–49)

Scripture #6

In Egypt we could eat all the fish we wanted, and there were cucumbers, melons, onions, and garlic. But we're starving out here, and the only food we have is the manna.

(Numbers 11:5–6)

Scripture #7

You may eat any animal that has divided hoofs and chews the cud. But you must not eat animals such as camels, rock badgers, and rabbits that chew the cud but don't have divided hoofs. And you must not eat pigs—they have divided hoofs, but don't chew the cud. All of these animals are unclean, and you are forbidden even to touch their dead bodies. You may eat anything that lives in water and has fins and scales. But it would be disgusting for you to eat anything else that lives in the water, and you must not even touch their dead bodies.

(Leviticus 11:2–12)

Scripture #8

Daniel made up his mind to eat and drink only what God had approved for his people to eat. And he asked the king's chief official for permission not to eat the food and wine served in the royal palace.

(Daniel 1:8)

Scripture #9

During the third year of his rule, Xerxes gave a big dinner for all his officials and officers. The governors and leaders of the provinces were also invited, and even the commanders of the Persian and Median armies came. For one hundred eighty days he showed off his wealth and spent a lot of money to impress his guests with the greatness of his kingdom.

(Esther 1:3–4)

Scripture #10

At the feast there were six stone water jars that were used by the people for washing themselves in the way that their religion said they must. Each jar held about twenty or thirty gallons. Jesus told the servants to fill them to the top with water.

Then after the jars had been filled, he said, "Now take some water and give it to the man in charge of the feast."

The servants did as Jesus told them, and the man in charge drank some of the water that had now turned into wine. He did not know where the wine had come from, but the servants did. He called the bridegroom over and said, "The best wine is always served first. Then after the guests have had plenty, the other wine is served. But you have kept the best until last!"

(John 2:6–10)

Scripture #11

About that time Emperor Augustus gave orders for the names of all the people to be listed in record books. These first records were made when Quirinius was governor of Syria. Everyone had to go to their own hometown to be listed. So Joseph had to leave Nazareth in Galilee and go to Bethlehem in Judea. Long ago Bethlehem had been King David's hometown, and Joseph went there because he was from David's family. Mary was engaged to Joseph and traveled with him to Bethlehem. She was soon going to have a baby, and while they were there, she gave birth to her first-born son. She dressed him in baby clothes and laid him on a bed of hay, because there was no room for them in the inn.

(Luke 2:1–7)

Scripture #12

They asked him, "Where do you want us to make preparations for it?" "Listen," he said to them, "when you have entered the city, a man carrying a jar of water will meet you; follow him into the house he enters and say to the owner of the house, 'The teacher asks you, "Where is the guest room, where I may eat the Passover with my disciples?"' He will show you a large room upstairs, already furnished. Make preparations for us there."

(Luke 22:9–12, NRSV)

Scripture #13

After saying this Jesus was troubled in spirit, and declared, "Very truly, I tell you, one of you will betray me." The disciples looked at one another, uncertain of whom he was speaking. One of his disciples—the one whom Jesus loved—was reclining next to him; Simon Peter therefore motioned to him to ask Jesus of whom he was speaking. (John 13:21–24, NRSV)

MILK and
HONEY
COOKING
SCHOOL

Recipes

PATRIARCHAL PERIOD

Goat Cheese Dip

6 ounces of feta cheese
2 cups Greek-style yogurt
2 tablespoons chopped dill
2 tablespoons chopped parsley
2 tablespoons chopped mint
2 tablespoons chopped walnuts (optional)

Cream together the feta cheese and the yogurt. Add the dill, parsley, and chopped mint. Serve on the Unleavened Bread. Serves enough for four tables.

Helpful Hint: Adding half a recipe more will make enough total for forty people to try a small amount.

Unleavened Bread

2 cups whole wheat flour
1 cup cold water
2 tablespoons olive oil
1 teaspoon salt

Combine flour, water, olive oil, salt. Form a dough. Knead for three minutes. Divide into eight balls and flatten into thin rounds. Prick with a fork. Cook on a griddle at 500 degrees for ten minutes. Makes about forty circles of bread.

Helpful Hint: Don't forget to double the recipe for use with the pottage.

Esau's Pottage

1 onion, chopped
1 tablespoon olive oil
1/2 teaspoon ground cumin
1/2 teaspoon ground coriander
2 cloves garlic, minced
3 cups chicken stock
1 cup red lentils
1/2 pound spinach (optional)
salt

Sauté onion in olive oil with cumin and coriander. Add the garlic at the last moment and brown. Add lentils and stock. Stir well and bring to a boil. Reduce heat and simmer forty-five minutes until lentils are tender. Cook ten minutes longer if necessary. Add spinach fifteen minutes before serving. Salt to taste. Feeds six.

Helpful Hint: Red lentils are difficult to find unless you have a Middle Eastern specialty grocer in your neighborhood. They aren't very red anyway, so substituting the regular lentils will hardly be noticed.

EGYPTIAN PERIOD

Challah Braid

Bread

2 packages yeast	3 cups bread flour
2 tablespoons sugar	2 teaspoons salt
3 tablespoons butter	2 eggs
1 cup of water	

Glaze
1 egg
1 teaspoon sugar
poppy seeds (optional)

Mix all the ingredients except the glaze ingredients in a large bowl to make a smooth elastic dough. Turn the dough out onto a floured surface and continue kneading for about ten minutes. (The surface will look blistered.) Return the dough to a bowl, cover with a dish towel, and leave it to rise for one hour. Punch down the dough and let it rest for fifteen minutes.

Divide the dough into three equal parts. Roll them into "snakes." Put them on a cookie sheet and join the three at the top. Loosely braid the three parts and then join them at the bottom. Cover the bread with a dish towel and let it rise in a warm place for forty-five minutes.

Heat the oven to 375 degrees. Beat the egg and one teaspoon sugar together and brush over the braid with a pastry brush. Option: Sprinkle with poppy seeds. Bake for forty-five minutes or until the top is lightly browned. One loaf serves twenty people. Make an extra loaf to show the group and then "break" in the traditional style.

BABYLONIAN PERIOD

Date Nut Halvah Balls

1/4 cup walnuts
1/3 cup almonds
4 oz dates, pitted
4 oz dried apricots
1/2 cup raisins
1/2 teaspoon cinnamon
1–2 tablespoons orange or lemon juice
1–2 teaspoons lemon zest

Chop the nuts in the food processor. Use short bursts with the food processor so that you get chopped nuts rather than pulverized ones. Cut the dates in half. Add the dates. raisins and cinnamon to the nut mixture. Add juice so that it sticks together. Add the lemon zest. Roll into small balls and serve. (One recipe makes forty small balls.)

Helpful Hint: This is one recipe that seems to be a hit with everyone. Make enough to have "seconds" and maybe even "thirds."

GREEK PERIOD

Honey Cheesecake

3 tablespoons pine nuts
2 cups ricotta cheese
1 cup honey
4 eggs, lightly beaten
3/4 teaspoon cinnamon
1 teaspoon lemon rind, grated
3 tablespoons almonds, slivered
1 whole wheat pie crust

Preheat oven to 350 degrees. Toast pine nuts on a baking sheet for five minutes. Mix cheese, honey, eggs, cinnamon, and lemon rind with a wire whisk. Chop the pine nuts and almonds and add to the mixture. (Note: Batter can be prepared by combining all ingredients in a food processor.) Pour into the whole wheat pie crust or into an oiled pie plate or spring-form pan. Bake for an hour and ten minutes. Refrigerate.

Helpful Hint: To save time and energy, you may purchase frozen cheesecake bites to substitute for this recipe.

NEW TESTAMENT PERIOD

Roman Bread Pudding

2 cups milk
1 loaf unsliced ciabatta bread
1 cup olive oil
honey

Pour milk into a mixing bowl. Cut the bread into bite-sized pieces and soak them in the milk. Move them around to make sure each piece has the same amount of milk soaked into it. In a frying pan, heat the olive oil over medium high heat. Put the milk-soaked bread into the frying pan and fry until golden brown on each side. Drizzle with honey and serve. This makes enough for twenty people to have a taste. For a bigger serving, double the recipe.

Haroset

6 apples, peeled and coarsely chopped
2/3 cup chopped almonds
3 tablespoons sugar
1/2 teaspoon cinnamon
grated rind of 1 lemon
4 tablespoons grape juice

Mix all the ingredients together thoroughly. Blend in a food processor until you reach the desired consistency. Chill. Serve with matzo crackers. This is enough for the whole group and then some.

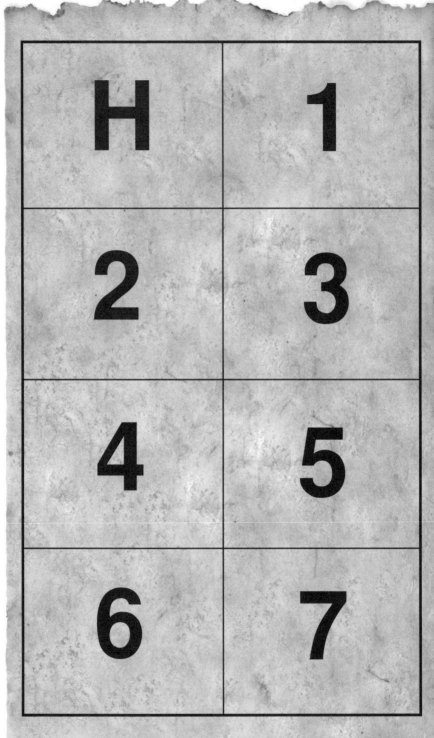

H	1
2	3
4	5
6	7

MILK AND HONEY COOKING SCHOOL

Appetizer
(Patriarchal Period)

Goat Cheese Dip

Unleavened Bread

Entree
(Patriarchal Period)

Esau's Pottage

Bread
(Egyptian Period)

Challah Braid

Fruit
(Babylonian Period)

Date Nut Halvah Balls

Dessert
(Greek/New Testament Period)

Honey Cheesecake

Roman Bread Pudding

Haroset (with matzo)

BIBLIOGRAPHY

Daily Life at the Time of Jesus by Miriam Vamosh (Abingdon Press, 2001). ISBN 0687048915.

Feast From the Mideast: 250 Sun-Drenched Dishes From the Lands of the Bible by Faye Levy (HarperCollins, 2003). ISBN 0060093617.

Food at the Time of the Bible by Miriam Vamosh (Abingdon Press, 2004). ISBN 0687340349.

The Good Book Cookbook, Recipes from Biblical Times by Naomi Goodman, Robert Marcus, and Susan Woolhandler (Dodd, Mead, and Company, 1986). ISBN 0396085784.

How People Lived in the Bible by Christa Kinde (Thomas Nelson, 2002). ISBN 0785242562.

Loaves of Fun: A History of Bread With Activities and Recipes From Around the World by Elizabeth M. Harbison (Chicago Review Press, 1997). ISBN 1556523114.

Manners and Customs in the Bible by Victor H. Matthews (Hendrickson Publishers, 1988). ISBN 094357577X.

Manners and Customs of Bible Lands by Fred H. Wight (Moody Press, 1983). ISBN 0802404163.